Anonymous

King Kalakaua's Tour Round the World

A sketch of incidents of travel

Anonymous

King Kalakaua's Tour Round the World
A sketch of incidents of travel

ISBN/EAN: 9783337212537

Printed in Europe, USA, Canada, Australia, Japan

Cover: Foto ©Andreas Hilbeck / pixelio.de

More available books at **www.hansebooks.com**

KING KALAKAUA'S

TOUR ROUND THE WORLD.

A SKETCH,

—— OF ——

INCIDENTS OF TRAVEL,

With a Map of the Hawaiian Islands.

——

PREPARED AND PUBLISHED

—— BY THE ——

P. C. ADVERTISER CO.,

No 23 Merchant Street,

Honolulu, H. I.

October 1881.

Jos. E. Wiseman, Advertising Agent, No. 27 Merchant Street,
Collected and Arranged the Advertisements in this Sketch.

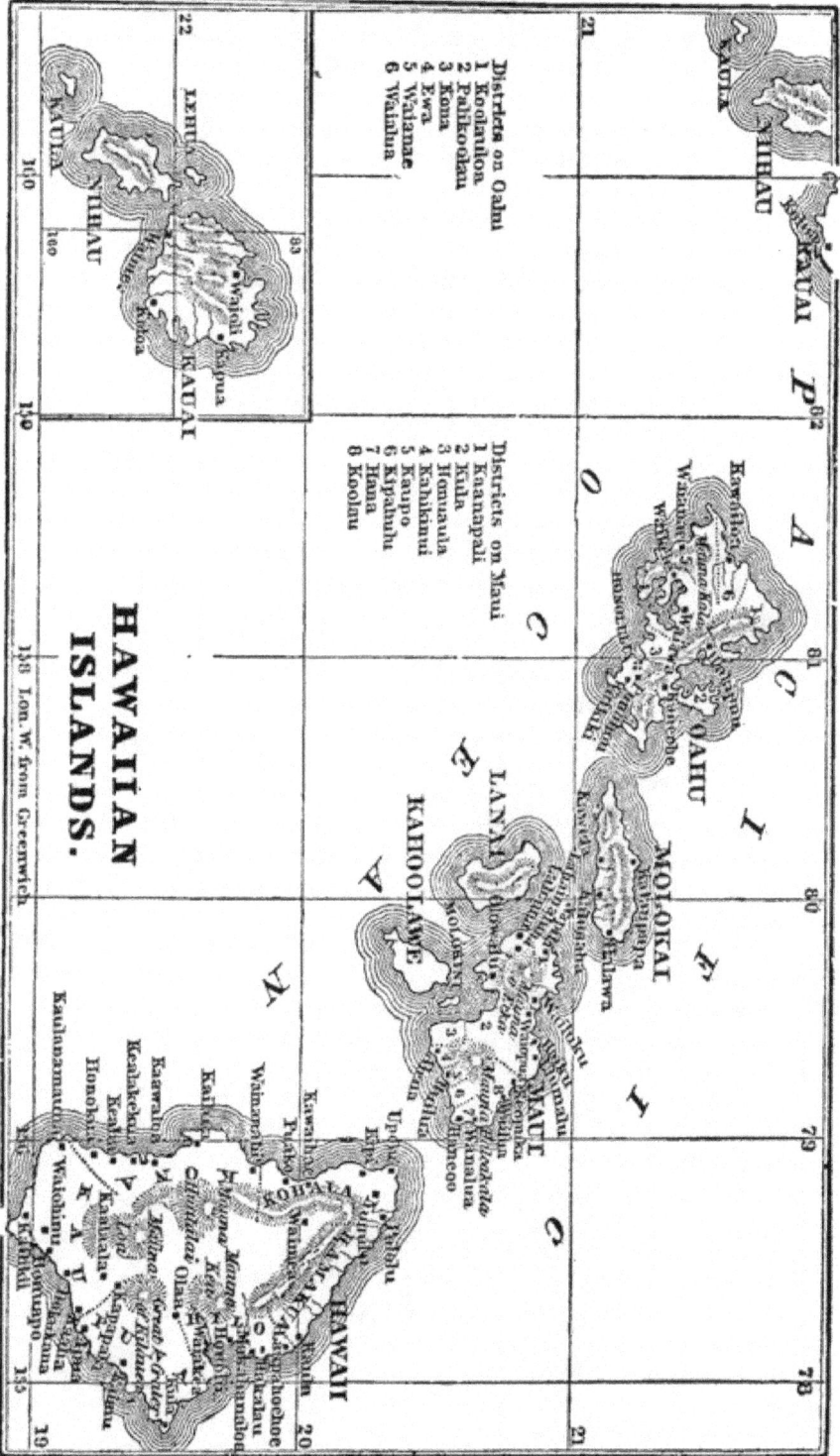
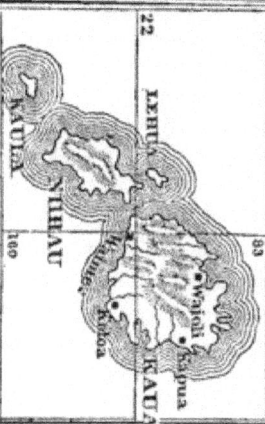

HAWAIIAN ISLANDS.

KING KALAKAUA'S
TOUR ROUND THE WORLD.

A SKETCH.

INTRODUCTION.

As the People of the Hawaiian Kingdom await with an affectionately loyal interest the return of their Sovereign from his tour round the world, it was to meet the expectation of the hour, that this slight sketch, or outline of His Majesty's travel was prepared; to be distributed on the day of the King's return to his capital, so that not only the Hawaiian resident, eager to recall to mind, the particulars of the royal journey, but also the stranger who might happen in our midst, should have in compact form, information of the King's movements abroad, and of the important objects, which animated a patriotic Hawaiian Chief to undertake the great journey.

About one year ago, the King's health had been unfavorably affected; and it was manifest, that a pleasant change, and complete relief from the cares of State, were necessary to restore His Majesty to his wonted vigor and healthful tone. But, King KALAKAUA, more alive to the interests of his State, than to the care of his person, would not consent to go abroad merely as an invalid tourist; but determined that his journey should be made subservient to the welfare of his Kingdom; and he undertook the arduous tour chiefly with a view to promote the re-population of his realm.

King KALAKAUA is the first and only Monarch who has made the tour of the world; and his journey was undertaken for the greatest and noblest purpose, that could animate a King. Looking to ancient times, we find a King of Ithaca who undertook an expedition to settle a point of honor, that affected his neighbor; or an Alexander who marched through Asia to leave a track of desolation behind; and in modern times, we see an adventuring Charles of Sweden, while madly seeking to destroy his neighbors, meet with his own destruction; or a Shah of Persia, traveling to squander barbaric wealth, and to display barbaric tastes; or an Emperor of Brazil, an enlightened and humane man; but who goes abroad to attend scientific congresses and gratify his taste for scientific lore; whereas our Hawaiian King,—our enlightened and humane Pacific Monarch, goes abroad solely for the purpose of benefitting his Kingdom, to promote the welfare of his people; and to make good the noble motto, and device, proclaimed at his accession,—"HOOULU LAHUI!"—INCREASE THE NATION!

HIS MAJESTY,

KING KALAKAUA,

Whose Kingdom comprises the Hawaiian Archipelago ; also Palmyra, Cornwallis, and other islands of the central Pacific, ascended the Throne, February 12th, 1874, and is the seventh Hawaiian monarch, since Kamehameha the Con. queror organized the Kingdom. His Majesty was born November 16, 1836, and is now in the forty-fifth year of his age and in the eighth of his reign. His Majesty received an excellent scholastic education in the Royal School, superintended by Rev. Mr. and Mrs. Cooke of the American Mission, in company with the late Kings Kamehameha IV. and V., King Lunalilo, Her Majesty Queen Dowager Emma, and other Princes and Princesses of the Kingdom. On leaving school, the young

Prince DAVID KALAKAUA was trained in military exercises. He received a commission as lieutenant of the King's Guard in 1852, was promoted Captain and Major on the accession of Kamehameha IV., and became Colonel and Chief of Staff, under Kamehameha V. His Majesty also filled the positions of Military Secretary and Lord Chamberlain, during the reigns of Kamehameha IV. and V. He was also member of the Privy Council of State, and hereditary Noble, or Alii of the House of Nobles. He ascended the Hawaiian Throne on the demise of King Lunalilo, in 1874 ; His Majesty speaks the English language with perfect purity, and has the style and manner of a highly cultivated gentleman. His Majesty is a very dilligent student, and has studiously perused the works of many modern thinkers of great eminence ; and as his tastes are decidedly military, His Majesty has a collection of military works, remarkable for variety and extent.

His Majesty, by invitation of the American Government, visited the United States in 1875. The Reciprocity Treaty of mutual advantage to the two countries was the result of the royal visit.

KING KALAKAUA'S BOAST.

O'er land and sea I've made my way
To farthest Ind, and great Cathay;
Reached Afric's shores, and Europe's strand;
And met the mighty of every land.
And as I stood by each sovereign's side,
Who ruled his realm with a royal pride,
I felt how small my sway,—and weak:—
My throne based on a mere volcanic peak,—
Where millions do these Kings obey,
Some thousands only own my sway.
And yet I feel that I may boast,
Some good within my sea-bound coast,
Richer than any of my grander peers.
That I within my realm need have no fears:—
May mingle with my people without dread;
No danger fear for my unguarded head,
And boast a treasure, sent me from above
That I have indeed, my people's love.

FAREWELL TO THE KING IN HIS CAPITAL.

A deep feeling of anxiety and interest pervaded the community on the eve of the departure of the King, and all classes and races strove to outvie each other in their expressions of good-will and affection, in bidding adieu to His Majesty. The loyal expression of the most intelligent foreign sentiment was manifested at the state dinner on Friday 13th Jan.; and on Sunday, the 16th the day was made memorable by an outpouring of affectionate adieux from His Majesty's native people. At the Catholic Cathedral High Mass was celebrated. The church was thronged with high officials, diplomatic attaches, and private citizens from every walk in life. The good Sisters of the Sacred Heart, preceded by their pupils, joined in this *bon voyage* to the King. The choir, reenforced for the occasion, rendered the selected music with tenderness and power. Monseigneur Bishop Louis Maigret with all the Fathers and Brothers of the order were present. After the sermon, the King with his escort and the Fathers, passed into the court-yard under an elevated alcove, when the following address was read to His Majesty by the Hon. Godfrey Rhodes:

To His Majesty the King :

SIRE:—We, your loyal and faithful subjects, are members of the Holy Catholic Church established in your Kingdom. And we, inspired by the uniform teachings of our Holy Religion, are imbued with a spirit of steadfast loyalty to your Majesty's person; as being appointed by Divine decree to the Sovereignty of the Hawaiian Islands; and when we receive assurances from your Majesty's lips of a contemplated purpose of travel in distant countries, even to the most distant, and to make a circuit of the Globe, we, in the spirit of faithful subjects, accept your Royal purpose, and are ready to unite in prayers to Almighty God to speed you on your way, and to preserve you in health 'till you return to your people. At the same time, prompted by our love to your Royal person, we feel constrained to say that your Majesty's departure at this time on so long a journey awakens our deep anxieties. We would be glad to have better assurances that your Majesty's safety and dignity abroad are fully provided for; and that the peace of the Kingdom will be fully assured during the absence of the King.

GOD SAVE YOUR MAJESTY.

Some words of warm adieu were uttered by native speakers. Enthusiasm, affection, and loyalty stirred the vast multitude, and plainly moved the heart of the King. Over one thousand people were present at the Cathedral.

AT KAWAIAHAO.

The old Stone Mission Church, a large audience assembled in the evening. The church was crowded to it's utmost capacity, and a warm and sympathetic feeling pervaded this mass of people, assembled to invoke the blessing of Almighty God in behalf of their King, about to take a long and perhaps a perilous journey. Their Majesties the King and Queen were present, also H. R. H. the Princess Liliuokalani, and other members of the Royal family.

The Rev. H. H. Parker opened the service of the evening with prayer, and after a melodious chant by a sweet-toned choir, His Majesty rose in his seat, and speaking of his intended departure, gave utterance to gracious words of hope and affection to his people; and he commended his royal sister, the Princess Liliuokalani to their generous and loyal care and support, to enable her to carry on satisfactorily the Government of the Kingdom during his absence. The words of His Majesty were received with warm and tender expressions of aloha and adieu.

At the conclusion of the King's remarks, the Hon. Noble Kapena rose to reply—

"We have heard our King tell us this evening about his intended visit abroad. He spoke to you from the same place six years ago, when he went before to visit America. It is true the King goes but for the good of his people, to make

ROYAL

HAWAIIAN HOTEL

HONOLULU.

Jno. M. Lawlor & Co.,

PROPRIETORS.

Hotel First Class in Every Respect.

Claus Spreckels. *Wm. G. Irwin.*

WM. G. IRWIN & Co.,
SHIPPING & COMMISSION
MERCHANTS.

Insurance and Plantation Agents.

CORNER QUEEN & FORT STS.,

Honolulu, H. I.

AGENTS FOR THE

Northwestern Mutual Life Insurance Co.

MILWAUKEE, WIS.,

Union Fire and Marine
Insurance Co.,

NEW ZEALAND.

Swiss Lloyds Marine Insurance Co.,

— AND —

San Francisco and Honolulu Packets.

the country richer by getting more capital and people to come this way. See the result of his visit to America—before he went natives were receiving but 25 cents per day, now see what they get, $2.50 and $3.00 per day. This is the King's work. New houses, ships, railroads, and every new enterprise are largely due to the King's visit abroad. But all this wealth is of no use if there is to be only one *kauna*, a mere handful of us left. So the King this time takes with him a Commissioner to enquire into and bring other people of brown skins here to re-people these isles. The King himself would be only so in name if he had no people to rule. The King will not rest until his hope of re-peopling these isles has been fulfilled. Let no one have any little feeling of jealousy about the King's going. Let no one be envious. The King goes to see how the great nations of the earth govern and rule their people, and it is well. It does not do to always remain in the dark. The great nations now look with respect on this little Kingdom and will have still more, when they see our King traveling among them for information to benefit his people. Let us all pray every day for the King's health, and safe return to his people."

MIDNIGHT SERENADES.

And the feelings of the people were not stayed from their expression, even after churches had closed, and the hours for slumber came; for, all night the Palace grounds were vocal with song and mele. At midnight and afterwards a band of Hawaiian chorus singers made the calm, clear moonlight vocal with tender and touching chant. Some of these choruses have a very sweet and plaintive melody; and during this lovely midnight hour, the soft summer air of the walks and umbrageous foliage of Iolani Palace, was tremulous with the tender songs of Hawaiians bidding farewell to their King.

THE KING AT SEA, ON THE "CITY OF SYDNEY."

His Majesty had a pleasant and interesting trip per "City of Sydney." The company on board was highly scientific. Professor Proctor discoursed to the King and other fellow passengers upon "Star depths," which have systems "inhabited by beings of greater importance than any that can be developed around our sun;" (of which beings we would like to

get an inkling, as to size and capacity) and he gave ample
assurances, that many remarkable planetary conjunctions of
this ill omened year, cannot have any appreciable terrestrial
influence; which was consoling to islanders on board, satisfy-
ing their minds that they would find their fast anchored
Archipelago on their return just where they left it. And
there was another scientist on board, Professor W. L. Car-
penter, who enlightened the royal party and other fellow travellers, with his views and experiences in relation to sea
depths and temperatures of the ocean; in which he explained
the laws affecting Gulf streams and ocean currents, and all
the natural phenomena of our quasi aqueous globe. He presented highly interesting illustrations of the infusorial life,
which he collected from the ooze of the ocean's bed at depths
of three, four and five miles, when he sailed with our friend
Sir Wyville Thompson on board the Challenger. He had
some of our globigerinæ to show, those infinitesimal crus-
taceæ which a pin point may cover, and are hardly visible to
the naked eye; yet reveal to the microscope a shelly buckler
upon which may be counted over eight hundred bosses each
covered with a multitude of figures and corrugations. After
one scientist had shown His Majesty remote suns so many
hundreds of million miles farther away from us than our own
sun, and so many thousands of millions of miles bigger than
our own globe, it was well that there was another scientist to
bring the King back to the earth, and mentally plunging with
him into the depths, could there reveal the infinitely small,
and bring the royal mind to a fine point.

To relieve this heavy strain of science, a vocalist on board
(G. Darrell, Esq.,) contributed some strains of song of love
and war for the entertainment of his fellow passengers. And
then comes the genial, social, and capable Captain Dearborn, to
add an inspiring word, and a cheering assurance, to make the
King and all his cabin happy.

It is stated by all on board during the trip, that
the voyage in respect to weather, and all other circumstances

was an exceedingly pleasant one. The King enjoyed himself in his usual cheerful and dignified, way, and seems to have won only golden opinions from all his fellow travelers.

On the morning of Thursday the 20th January, the City of Sydney steamed away from Honolulu with the royal party; and on the afternoon of Saturday the 29th, she steamed into the harbor within the Golden Gate. And now we will quote from the chroniclers of San Francisco and Sacramento, other particulars attending the King's tour round the world.

THE KING IN SAN FRANCISCO.

His Majesty was right royally received by the citizens of San Francisco. The ladies of the Palace Hotel determined to tender to the monarch a reception in the parlors of the hotel, ere he departed upon his tedious ocean voyage to the Flowery Kingdom. Gigantic efforts were put forth by the ladies, and everything done that could add one *iota* to the perfection of detail or brilliancy of the whole fete. Last evening the auspicious event transpired, and a grander reception it has seldom, if ever, been allotted to a San Franciscan to witness. The ladies of the Invitation and Reception Committees may rest satisfied with their well earned laurels. The arrangements were simply perfect; the lists of guests was taken from the *creme de la creme* of our ˙society, and the judgment of the delighted guests was a unanimous verdict of praise. The most wonderful circumstance in connection with last evening's affair was the astonishing rapidity with which the whole had been elaborated since the inception, scarce one short week ago, and adds one more to the honors of the Committees.

The cards of invitation were engraved in script, on a heavy card, four by five and a quarter inches, and read as follows :

The Ladies of the Palace Hotel
request the pleasure of your company
Monday Evening, February Seventh,
at eight o'clock,
To Meet His Majesty, King Kalakaua.

RECEPTION COMMITTEE:

Mrs. F. G. Newlands,	Mrs. J. S. Hager,
Mrs. Howard Colt,	Mrs. H. Schmiedell,
Mrs. A. G. Kinsey,	Mrs. W. H. L. Barnes,
Mrs. Mark Severance,	Mrs. J. Lugsain.

"The reception will long be rememberd by the fortunate guests, who were permitted to witness this one of the grandest social events in the history of the city."

KING KALAKAUA ENTERTAINED AT THE PACIFIC YACHT CLUB HOUSE.

Although His Majesty, King Kalakaua did not come here in his official capacity, he has received attentions from our citizens as numerous as on his previous visit six years ago.

The distinguished visitors have no cause to complain of the hospitality of their friends in this city, as the latter apparently vie with one another in their attentions to the King and his suite. The fact that His Majesty is travelling incognito has been taken advantage of by some of his friends to give entertainments which they believe will be of special interest to him, when formality, due to a King, but which can be waived in the person of a Prince, does not interfere with the pleasures of their guests, Such an affair took place yesterday afternoon, when Commodore R. S. Floyd, of the Pacific Yacht Club, gave an informal entertainment in honor of His Majesty. Commodore Floyd is one of those gentlemen who has enjoyed several years of warm personal friendship with

M. S. GRINBAUM & CO.

IMPORTERS & COMMISSION

MERCHANTS.

---

38 QUEEN ST., : *HONOLULU H. I.*

M. S. GRINBAUM & CO.

IMPORTERS AND COMMISSION

MERCHANTS.

---

214 California St., San Francisco, Cal.

King Kalakaua, and yesterday he invited the latter to a sail on the bay and a dinner at the Club House, near Saucelito.

Capt. Menzies took occasion to express the honor the members of the Club felt in entertaining such a distinguished guest, and proposed the toast of His Majesty, King Kalakaua. The King responded briefly, returning thanks to Commodore Floyd and the members of the Pacific Yacht Club for the elegant entertainment and for their action in electing him a member of the Club which he considered a great honor, and would always remember the whole affair as one of the most pleasant incidents of his visit to San Francisco. He also expressed the hope that on his return next August that he would again have the pleasure of meeting the members of the Club on such an occasion, with the additional attraction of the presence of the ladies. His remarks were warmly applauded, and at their conclusion rousing cheers were given.

THE CHINESE CONSUL-GENERAL'S DINNER TO KING KALAKAUA.

The Chinese Consul-General entertained King Kalakaua with a dinner at the Hang Fer Low restaurant, the Delmonico of Chinatown, last evening. In a Celestial way it was a very swell affair. All the nobs of Chinatown were there in their best bibs and tuckers. The company outside of the state table included the President and Secretary of each of the nine Chinese Benevolent Associations of the city and all of the rich wholesale merchants, to the number of sixty. They wore an extraordinary costume for the occasion, being dressed in mandarin rank, with buttons and other insignia to denote their standing. The buttons are worn in their caps, the color denoting the rank of their blue-blood wearers. The majority wore the crystal button, a few the red, the latter indicating the bluest of the blue bloods. The restaurant, which is orientally gorgeous in its appointments, was splendidly decorated for the occasion, and its usual display of gas

jets being supplemented with an abundance of large vari-
colored lanterns of paper and bamboo, gave it a brilliant
aspect viewed from the street or the surrounding houses.
The royal table was spread in the small room of the restaurant, which was specially dressed for the occasion.

THE GUESTS.

On the wall at the foot of the table, facing the Consul
General, who presided, were festooned the American, Chinese and Hawaiian flags. Around the regal board were
gathered the King, the Consul, the principal members of the
Consulate, the traveling companions of the King, and such
of our citizens as were invited. On the landing they were
drawn up in a line, and the Chinese, after making a concerted
salaam and shaking each his own hand, after their sociable
custom, were brought forward and each in turn was presented
to the King, shaking his hand and passing to each member
of the party. This little reception, in which the Chinese
shewed an easy, polished politeness, over, the festal party
was seated. The persons named above were seated at the
State table, the others in the adjoining room about little
square tables, each accommodating five guests, the outer side
of the table being left unoccupied, in order that its hanging
of rich crimson satin with gold embroidery might be shown
to advantage. The feasting done, Colonel Bee arose, and on
behalf of the Consul-General proposed the health of the King,
saying that the entertainment had been devised from a desire
to show him some of the inner life of the Chinese, and to
wish him a prosperous and pleasant journey. They desire
that the three flags entwined on the wall should represent
the three countries which the Pacific ocean divided, yet
brought close together, joined in amity for all time ; that
they might go hand in hand, prosperous in all the arts and
sciences, civilization, and everything that makes nations and

ROBESON & SORENSON,
Civil, Naval & Military
TAILORS.

Co-Operative Tailoring Establishment,
Fort Street, Honolulu, H. I.

NEW IMPORTATIONS OF GOODS
Constantly Arriving

From Foreign Manfacturers, Carefully Selected to Suit the Trade.

Prices Always Reasonable.

HEBBARD,

DRAY & EXPRESSMAN
GOODS DELIVERED PROMPTLY,
On Reasonable Terms.

Office, 69 1+2 King Street.

To all who wish strict attention paid to their business in my line. I will endeavor at all times to give most careful consideration.

PATRONAGE SOLICITED FROM THE OTHER ISLANDS.

VISIT TO SACRAMENTO.

King Kalakaua in the Capital City of California—He visits the Legislature and takes in several other sights—The Governor chaperons him about the city.

Quite a large crowd had collected at the depot to see this genuine, living representative of modern monarchy, who proved to be a rather portly and generally fine-looking man of middle age, dressed in plain citizen's garb, and sporting a pretty fair set of side-whiskers. His countenance bore a genial expression, and the impression that one could get from a brief glance at the royal gentleman would be a favorable one.

TAKING IN THE TOWN.

The royal party was accompanied from San Francisco by Hon. Claus Spreckels. Carriages were in waiting for them, to which they were promptly conducted and driven rapidly to the Capitol, where an informal visit was paid to His Excellency Governor Perkins, and a brief time was spent in pleasant conversation. Apartments had been secured for the party at the Arcade Hotel, to which they repaired at the conclusion of their visit to the Governor, the Governor accompanying them, the latter having accepted an invitation from His Majesty to dine with him. An elegant dinner was partaken of, after which the King expressed a desire to visit a theater, and it was accordingly arranged that the party should drop in at the Capital varieties, the only place of amusement now open in this city, where three private boxes were placed at their disposal. During the evening several calls were made upon prominent citizens, His Majesty retiring a little before midnight.

To-day the party again visited the State Capitol, and spent
4

considerable time on the floor of each House, in the proceedings of which they seemed to take much interest.

King Kalakaua is traveling incognito, his trip having no official significance, and being merely for the purpose of observation and pleasure. For this reason he is addressed as Prince by his traveling companions.

His Majesty returned to San Francisco the following day.

OTHER ENTERTAINMENTS OF THE KING IN SAN FRANCISCO.

THE FRENCH BALL.—Platt's Hall was crowded to its utmost capacity on Saturday evening last, where the Ligue Nation. ale Francaise gave a reception in honor of the new French Consul, M. Vauvert de Mean and Madame Mean. His Majesty, King Kalakaua, accompanied by Colonel Judd and Major Macfarlaine of his staff were present. In the first Lancers, His Majesty danced with Madame Planet, wife of the French Chancellor, and subsequently waltzed with Mrs. Dr. Julius Rosenstin. Later in the evening he escorted the latter lady to supper.

The King evidently enjoyed the affair, as he participated in most of the dances after supper.

His Majesty was entertained at dinner by Claus Spreckels, Esq.; a very grand banquet, prepared in the highest style of Parisian art, and the most prominent men of the city were invited to join the King.

Another delightful entertainment in honor of the King, a soiree musicale gotten up by our Consul Mr. Severance at the Palace Hotel. This is reported as an exquisite affair of lyrical entertainment, and was attended by the elite of the city.

Thus every day, and it may be said every hour of King Kalakaua's stay in San Francisco has been filled up with a

W. E. FOSTER.

WHO KEEPS CONSTANTLY ON HAND

Light Single and Double Harness,
Heavy Single and Double Harness,
Concord Double Harness,
Mule Plow Harness,
Mule Cart Harness,
Sydney Saddles,
Mexican Saddles,
Saddle Bags.
Whips, Curry Combs, Brushes,

And all other articles used in the Horse Line too numerous to mention.

The only Shop which keeps a supply of Prof.
Going's Remedies for Horse and
Mule Diseases.

— ALSO —

Head Quarters for the Artesian Ice Works,
which expect to keep the city of Honolulu
cool with Pure Artesian Ice

Orders from the other Islands Promptly Attended to

81 FORT ST., HONOLULU.

grand ovation of festivities. And we feel assured that no
potentate of Europe, nor eminent great man of America's
own soil, could have received greater and more honorable
attention; and as the San Francisco *Call* says this is accorded
to King Kalakaua, because as a worthy Chief, he has won
the love of a loyal people.

THE KING'S POPULARITY ABROAD.

"King Kalakaua has been entertained right royally by
our social lions since his re entry into San Francisco society,
and can hardly feel otherwise than pleased at the marks of
esteem that he is everywhere receiving. That His Majesty
had a right to expect an ovation, his previous visit assured
him, still he must have been unprepared for the very generous outpouring of hospitality that has greeted him. This
lionizing is not so much the outcome of a desire to honor the
rank of the royal visitor, as an admiration of him who has
done so much in one short reign towards the social and
political advancement of his people; a people whom he
found, on coming into his heritage, to be very far down in
the scale of nations. That the ruler of the Sandwich Islands
is to-day feted the world over, is an all-sufficient argument as
to the success of his earnest efforts ; hence these tokens of
respect."

On the 8th inst., His Majesty and suite went on board the
steamship Oceanic, accompanied by a host of enthusiastic
friends, and sailed for Japan and various ports of Asia.

VOYAGE ON THE OCEANIC.

Among the incidents of the journey of His Majesty, when
at sea on board the *Oceanic*, and sailing across the meridian
of Honolulu but a few degrees to the northward of this
Archipelago; conversation of the Royal party and travelling

friends, turned upon the home feeling that sprung up in Hawaiian hearts, yearning for their own loved shores, when thus passing them by, as it were. And His Majesty touched with reminiscences of his Kingdom, his people and his Queen, especially the latter, gave such a tender expression to his home and domestic feelings, that a little poetic inspiration, there and then present, shaped the faithful, royal emotion into the following lines. They were a waft of emotion from the King on the high sea, not only to His Queen, but also to all His people.

SONNET.

KALAKAUA TO KAPIOLANI.

(*The Island King to His Queen.*)

WRITTEN ON BOARD THE OCEANIC, FEB. 16, 1881.

On the meredian of Honolulu. In lat. 38°; lon. 157°, 30'.

1

To catch a glimpse of yonder shore,
  My eager eyes I strain,
And pray that I was there—once more!
  Let me not pray in vain !

2

The surf it's silvery crests display,
  On that far shore I love,
When back, I make my homeward way,
  No more I'll care to rove.

3

Dear waiting one, I think of thee,
  The maile round thy neck !
O, tell me, wild and angry sea,
  How long you'll hold me back ?

4

Since, then I cannot meet you now,
  Divided by the main,
Let me tell you fondly how,
  I hope we'll meet again.

5

A love like thine, so leal and true,
  My devious way will guard;.
And when the rounded world I view,
  Thy love is my reward.

ESTABLISHED IN 1847.

BOLLES & CO.,

SHIP CHANDLERS,

Commission Merchants.

IMPORTERS AND DEALERS IN

General Merchandise.

No. 35, Queen Street, Honolulu, H. I.

Agents for the Sale of all kinds of Hawaiian Produce.

Country Orders Faithfully Executed.

LAINE & CO.,

COMMISSION MERCHANTS,

AND INPORTERS AND DEALERS IN

Hay, Grain and General Produce,

HONOLULU, H. I.

THE ROYAL HOTEL,

J. WELSH, : : Manager,

Cor. Nuuanu & Merchants Sts., Honolulu. H. I.

DEALERS IN AND IMPORTERS OF THE

Best Wines, Spirits, Ales, Porters, &c.

TO BE FOUND IN THE CITY.

Billiard Parlors attached to the House, and every attention paid to our Patrons.

VISIT TO JAPAN.

ARRIVAL AT YOKOHAMA.

As the *Oceanic* steamed into Yokohama harbor very early on the morning of the 4th March, the eager lookout from the decks of the steamer could count forty-two men-of-war and large steamers at anchor in the bay. The Hawaiian flag had been run up to the main and had floated in the morning breeze but a few moments, when a brilliant display of bunting arched each giant ship-of-war and steamer, from the water's edge to the main truck, and from main truck to water's edge, with the flag of Hawaii flying at the main of *every one*. At the same time the shrill boatswains whistles piped lively over the waters, as the nimble tars coursed up riging and, swarming out on the yards of their several ships, manned them in splendid style, and hurrahed, not only three times three, but all the time whilst our steamer was passing in review, and ships and shore joined with guns in a royal roar of welcome.

Hardly had the *Oceanic* anchored, when hundreds of sampans, or native canoes, and small craft of all kinds, came thronging around the broad sides of the great steamer, and the people on board this mosquito fleet were making a clamor that drowned the shrieks of the steamer's whistle, when a shot was heard, a puff of smoke was observed to float away from a distant battery, a steam launch put off, and by magic, as it were, the clamor outside the *Oceanic* had ceased, and the swarming sampans had pulled and paddled out of sight. The approaching launch bore a forked white flag with a red ball in the centre and an Imperial crown on top. This was the Imperial launch with the Admiral on board. The royal standard of Hawaii was now run up to the main. Again a

5

grand salvo pealed forth from every war-ship, and chief an-swered chief right royally in Yokohama bay.

Admiral Nakamura of the Royal Japanese Navy, came on board, and communicating with the gentlemen of His Majesty's suite, conveyed to them His Imperial Majesty's wish that his royal brother of Hawaii would be the guest of the Sovereign of Japan during all of his stay on Japanese soil.

His Majesty consented to waive his incognito and become the guest of the Emperor of Japan, as King of the Hawaiian Islands.

Eight state boats or barges, followed the steam launch, and bore the King and suite with baggage and attendants to the Imperial summer seat Noge Yama.

As the royal party landed and proceeded on their way, they were greeted on all sides with enthusiastic demonstrations of welcome. At every crossing they past, along two miles of route, the Japanese and the Hawaiian flags were suspended from lofty poles on either side, that leaned over almost touch-ing trucks, so that the Imperial white banner and the cross and bars of Hawaii, blended their folds together over the heads of the passing cortege.

SUMMER PALACE OF NOGEYAMA.

After a ceremonious reception at the grand entrance of the Palace, His Majesty was escorted to magnificent chambers and parlor, used as Imperial apartments, that were superbly tapestried, with ebony and gold furniture, with most elabor-ate arabesques, with palatial chandeliers, with doors of enamel and gold; and the burnished gold and glossy lacquered and enameled surfaces reflected the surprise and delight of our royal party.

· His Majesty's suite were also provided with apartments in the Palace.

Prince Higashi-Fushimi-no-Miya, waited on our travellers.

HONOLULU & SAN FRANCISCO
Express Company.

San Francisco Office, : : No. 110 Sutter St.
Honolulu Offices, : : : No. 94 King St.
(One Door above Fort Street.)

AND HAWAIIAN HOTEL.
H. H. WEBB, Manager and Proprietor.

This General Transportation Express Business

SO, RECENTLY STARTED IS

Meeting with Wonderful Success,

AND MAKES IT A

Great Benefit to the Community

— IN —

Shipping Merchandise, Treasure, Packages, And Baggage

To and From San Francisco and Honolulu

Island Agencies Established on Hawaii
and Maui, at Hilo and Wailuku.

SPECIAL ATTENTION GIVEN TO CITY AND ISLAND TRADE

Advances made on Consignments, Collections
and Commissions Solicited and
Promptly Attended to

All Vessels coming and going are visited by my
several Express Wagons.

He pointed out the marvels of the Imperial summer seat, and as the royal party expressed their unqualified delight; they were assured that this was but the threshold of the Imperial palatial glories.

The royal party after spending the night at Nogeyama, the Imperial summer seat, left Yokohama the following day at 11 o'clock A. M., by express train for Tokio, distant 18 miles, and on arrival were received by four Imperial Princes, who accompanied His Majesty and suite to the Palace. His Imperial Japanese Majesty met King Kalakaua in the ante hall of the Palace, and welcomed him to Japan with marked cordiality. The King was then conducted to the saloon of the Empress, where he was received with distinguished courtesy and amicable attention. After a few hours repose, His Majesty the King, was informed by an Imperial Prince of His Imperial Majesty's approach, to return the visit of the King of Hawaii in his apartments.

PALACE OF ENRIOKWAN.

Our Hawaiian royal party were highly impressed with the admirable order of the Imperial Palace at Tokio. The magnificent park grounds seemed to be swarming with attendants, and all dressed in European fashion, of good style and quality of garments. An admirable system of service seemed to regulate the government of the palace. Everybody and everything scrupulously clean, and all work and service carried on without any noise or confusion.

On the morning after arrival at Tokio the Hawaiian visitors were surprised to find that a fall of snow, had occured during the night, to the depth of 4 inches, and had covered the Palace Park with a complete mantle of white. Soon they observed some laborers with pieces of matting about 6 feet long, and with pieces of bamboo at each end, a simple contrivance for removing rubbish, and in a few hours, not a speck of snow was to be seen in the park.

This beautiful palace is shaped like a letter H, with a central line of edifice, and two wings of about the same length. The Imperial walls are black, and black and gold in glossy, enamel appear everywhere, as the expression of Japanese Imperial taste. The walls of the palace chambers are not papered, but draped or tapestried with exquisite patterns of muslin and silk. Superb ebony and gold wardrobes and beaufets, adorn the spacious chambers and parlors. English fire-grates, with polished marble or steel mantels are in all the apartments. Numerous French and Swiss clocks of beautiful and elaborate designs, afford ample opportunity to note the flight of time in this palace of delights.

One thing of beauty especially attracted the attention of our royal tourists, was the regal Camelia, so superb and perfect in its choosen home. In all parts of the palace upon etageres and stately beaufets, they beheld lofty lacquered vases, in which were camelias, as large as saucers, cream tinted and waxen white, like marvellous productions of the most consummate art. This royal flower ought to attain all its perfection of beauty in Hawaii nei, and we hope that one of the results of His Majesty's visit to Japan, will be the cultivation of the camelia ; so that should a Japanese Emperor, or Imperial Prince come this way, they will be pleased to be greeted by the queenly flower of their own home. Also a wonderful variety of miniature plants in vases the size of a teacup ; and a great taste, and elegance of horticulture, were everywhere observed.

In one chamber, the King and suite found four perfect billiard tables of the latest patterns set apart for their use. In another apartment a grand piano of the finest tone. Pictures, objects of virtu, bric a brac, and curios of the rarest quality in great profusion. And the physical comforts of the travellers were admirably provided for. Fanciful dishes, yet of excellent taste, were in profusion on the dining table ; and in their private rooms, each one of the party found costly lacquered trays loaded with a variety of bonbons, which they supposed could not be found outside of Paris. All the table service used was of solid gold or silver ware.

HYMAN BROTHERS,

—IMPORTERS OF—

GENERAL MERCHANDISE

——o:FROM:o——

FRANCE, GERMANY, ENGLAND AND AMERICA.

29 Merchant St., Honolulu, H. I.

HYMAN BROTHERS,

WHOLESALE GROCERS,

216 & 218 California St., San Francisco, Cal.

Special Attention Paid to Orders from the

SANDWICH ISLANDS,

POSSESSING A THOROUGH KNOWLEDGE OF

THAT TRADE.

Family Grocery & Feed Store,

ODD FELLOW'S HALL BUILDING,

93 & 95 FORT STREET, HONOLULU, H. I.

A. W. BUSH,

IMPORTER OF AND DEALER IN

CHOICE TEAS,

SHIP, PLANTATION, FAMILY

AND PASSENGER STORES, ETC.

Orders from the other Islands will at all times receive my prompt and careful attention. Special attention given to Naval Stores of every Description, both Cabin and otherwise. All description of Horse and Cattle Feed constantly on hand. Goods carefully packed for shipment, and warranted. Goods carried free of charge to all parts of the City.

New Goods Received By Every Packet.

BILLS COLLECTED MONTHLY.

SHINTOMIZA THEATRE.

On the day following their arrival, the royal party were escorted to the Imperial Theatre, Shintomiza. Twenty-eight carriages were required to take the train of Imperial Princes and Princesses, and high dignitaries, who formed the escort of His Majesty the King. One thousand globe shaped lanterns were displayed in front of and around the theatre ; and each one had the Imperial Japanese flag, and the Royal Hawaiian standard painted on them. Every walk, and every tree in the spacious theatre garden was hung with illuminated globes, every corridor and lobby was lined with them ; and the interior of the theatre was in a blaze of light.. It was estimated that over 3000 of these brilliant illuminated lanterns decorated the great theatre, and were an especial display, marvellous even to Japanese eyes, in honor of King Kalakaua's visit.

The centre of the dress circle, an Imperial reservation, capable of seating 50 persons, was fitted up and decorated most superbly. The programme in English and Japanese printed on white satin with gold fringe, the Japanese Imperial and the royal Hawaiian flags *interwoven* in colors. The Imperial and Royal Standards decorating the centre of the circle; and also the front of the stage. Elaborate lacquered tables were placed before the royal party, and loaded with sweetmeats, and cordials and cigars; all the gentlemen smoking, and indulging in a pose of ease and sans facon, not permitted at the Palace. His Majesty was in evening full dress, and decorated with the star of the order of Kalakaua. The Princes present each wore a single star of decoration.

The impression produced by this audience of wealthy Japanese, was that a high order of intelligence pervaded the company. A large number of spectacles and eyeglasses were observed, on what appeared to be very, studious faces. All

6

well dressed, and no vulgar, or clamorous applauding or his. sing.

The make up and personal appearance of the Princesses there present, called forth some enthusiastic remarks from the travellers. They are described as having very fair, pearly and transparent complexions, with high arched eyebrows, a great sweetness and beauty of expression, and dressed very tastefully in soft, yet brilliant silks; and with a dazzling sparkle of brilliants around their beautiful necks, and in the lobes of their shell tinted ears.

On the stage, our travellers saw fairies floating through the air like butterflies, and a terrific giant fighting with about fifty warriors; and His Majesty was delighted with the oddity and marvelous variety of the performance.

During His Majesty's stay in Kioto he ordered to be presented in his name; and as a souvenir of the royal Hawaiian visit to the Japanese Capital, a drop curtain for the great Shintomiza Theatre. In the month of July subsequent to His Majesty's visit, the curtain was finished and presented to manager Morita by Hawaiian Consul Robert Irwin Esq. in behalf of His Majesty.

The curtain is of crimson Japanese velvet. The Hawaiian Royal Coat of Arms is embroidered in gold in the centre, and distributed on each side of this in white silk embroidery is the inscription, 'Presented to the Shintomiza Theatre by Kalakaua the First, King of Hawaii, in the second month of the year 2541 (Japanese era).' The curtain was manufactured by Nishimaru & Co., of Kiyoto, and is, the handsomest thing of the kind that has ever been used in a Japanese Theatre.

What an advertisement of the little Kindom, in that great empire, is this drop curtain? The multitudes of Kioto assemble in this great theatre that seats 5000 people,—not only to look upon exhibitions of Japanese mimic art; but also to listen at times to Christian teachers; and as they gaze during

the periods of intermission upon the name, and blazoury of King Kalakaua and his kingdom, what feelings of interest and curiosity must be evoked; and what prestige for little Hawaii, thus promoted by the intelligent courtesy of her thoughtful and patriotic chief abroad!

STATE DINNER AT AKASAKA PALACE.

A succeeding day, His Imperial Majesty of Japan, entertained His Hawaiian Majesty at a grand state dinner, for which 238 covers were laid. On this occasion all the Imperial Princes and Princesses, of the court were present.

The bill of fare was printed on white satin, with fringe of gold, and with the Hawaiian coat of arms at top wrought with gold thread.

The table service gold and silver. The spoons and ladles of gold, and other articles of the service had the Imperial Japanese and Hawaiian flags graven upon them, *with the Hawaiian crown on top.*

When some rare and costly Veuve Clicquot, a present from the Emperor of Russia, was uncorked, the health of His Majesty the King of the Hawaiian Islands was proposed by His Imperial Japanese standing. The band struck up at the time the Hawaiian anthem, and the toast was received with the most distinguished honors by the illustrious company present. His Majesty did not respond by proposing His Imperial Majesty's health, as some present expected; because His Majesty bearing in mind that the Emperor would lunch with him on the morrow, thought that then would be the proper occasion to return the compliment. His Majesty's appreciation of a correct etiquette was fully recognized.

In the centre of the great banquetting table was a fountain all gold, of the most exquisite workmanship, with Japanese designs of dragons and fantastic figures of gods and goddesses, but it was not playing. His Imperial Majesty in the course of conversation with the King, expressed regret that the fountain had recently met with an accident in its hydraulic works, it was an intricate piece of machinery and was out of order, and he was sorry to say, would not sport its diversified jets as usual. His Majesty quickly responded that the High Powers of heaven had been pouring out such a superabundance of water of late (recent heavy rains) to bless and fructify His Imperial Majesty's domains, that the little gods and goddesses of the fountain felt, no doubt, that it would be impious to add their little spout at this time. His Imperial Majesty laughed heartily at the conceit, and the remark and the mirth went the round of the assembled dignitaries.

His Majesty the King accepted an invitation to visit the First Christian Church of Yokohama on their anniversary, the tenth of March, to which the people of his Kingdom had so liberally contributed, many years ago.

On the afternoon of March 12th, His Majesty the King was received in grand audience by His Majesty the Emperor, at the Private Palace; the Imperial Princes and Princesses in attendance. It was the occasion of the presentation to the Emperor of the portrait of His Majesty the King, and of Her Majesty Queen Kapiolani.

His Majesty the King was presented with two Japanese armors of ancient style, made of the best steel; visors and all polished; very curious, and of largest size. His Majesty the King received a multitude of presents from various quarters.

When the King and his suite visited the Enriokwan Mansion, in a grand park, in Tokio, the grounds were illuminated by over 4,000 Japanese globe lanterns; and the King and suite were robed in very rich Japanese court costumes, provided expressly for this occasion.

On the 14th of March the King was presented with the grand cross of the Imperial Japanese order of Kris-anthemum, by the hands of His Imperial Majesty of Japan; and on the 15th the Emperor lunched with the King, and was decorated by His Majesty of Hawaii with the Grand Cross of Kamehameha.

We have only glanced at many interesting and important

incidents during the King's sojourn of ten days, given in addition to those we clip from Yokohama foreign journals, whilst a guest of the Emperor of Japan at Tokio; and many we must pass by for the present. Some incidents attending the King's departure from Hawaii; the loyal ovation of Kohalans; and especially the incident of the bearing of the King on the shoulders of his people, through the surf by torchlight, were discussed in the grand banqueting hall of the Palace of Akasaka ; and the ADVERTISER, of Honolulu, that had been thoughtfully transmitted to, and carefully read by, gentlemen of the Imperial household, was quoted as authority in speaking of the story. His Imperial Majesty was much gratified to be informed of this demonstration of enthusiastic loyalty to his royal guest, when at home.

THE KING VISITS A MISSIONARY MOTHER.

His Majesty was invited to a grand festivity at Yokohama, where many European as well as Japanese high officials had assembled to meet King Kalakaua; but His Majesty awakened much surprise, and a feeling of increased respect for Christian Missionary workers, in the minds of the Japanese, by deferring his attendance at the great festivity, and by calling upon old lady Gulick, the Missionary mother residing in Yokohama, whilst the assembled distinguished guests awaited His Majesty's presence.

VISIT TO KOBE.

King Kalakaua sailed from Yokohama, the 16th March on board the steamship Tokio Maru. His Majesty was accompanied on the journey by the Princes and Daimios, who had been commanded by the Emperor to attend upon the King as especial escort, during every hour of his stay in Japan. The courtesy and royal attention shown to the King in Japan, recals the spirit of princely courtesy of the noblest days of the

7

mediœval chivalry of Christendom.　Hawaii is placed under
deep obligation to Japan.

The royal party arrived at Kobe on the 18th March—and
were received by the Governor of the City with ceremonious
attention.　His Majesty rested a short while at the Governor's
residence; and during his short stay visited a grand and ancient palace, and one of the extensive temples of Japan.　The
palace of Kobe is surrounded by a wall 12 feet high and 3 feet
wide at the top.　In the great audience Hall is a throne of
large dimension and singular structure.　In the center of the
Hall is a raised square of dais, of gold and vermillion lacquer.
This is covered with a canopy of heavy embroidered silk of
the richest quality.　In the centre of the dais is a throne
chair, of brilliant gold and vermillion lacquer; and the roof of
this stately hall is supported by 12 lofty smooth columns, or
resplendent shafts with surfaces of polished gold.　On each
side of the dais, are suspended picture of the Emperor and
the Empress of Japan.　All the doors of the palace are
frames covered with pictured tapestry, and are moved in
grooves or slides.　The royal party noticed a beautiful miniature lake in the palace grounds, enclosed by box bush shrubbery.　A narrow causeway, shaded with the rarest shrubbery
leads to a rock in the centre of the pellucid lake.　This rock
is overgrown with mosses and creepers, and has a delightful
cool grotto recess; and in this sweet spot, whose sacred priv-
acy is only invaded by the lake carp, or the Japanese thrush,
their Imperial Majesties of Niphon come to cool their sacred
persons during the summer solstice.

At the Buddhist temple, a grand and gloomy structure,
two dozen priests robed in vari colored silks and gold, received the King and suite.　The royal party were conducted into
the presence of the collossal images of Buddha; the Badiva
or Sacred Parent of the ancient Asiatic world.　Our travellers were allowed to gaze a short while but not to enter the
recesses where the god and the symbolic dragon were placed.

THE ROYAL SHAVING

—· AND —

Hair Dressing Parlors

AND BATH ROOMS,

GEO. VOGT, Proprietor, No. 82 Hotel Street,.
Honolulu, H. I.

I call the attention of the public to my new place of business, recently fitted up with enlarged facilities, where I am prepared to give special attention to

Barbering, Hair Cutting, Dying, Hair Werk, &c.

My BATH ROOMS adjoining are superior to any in the Islands.
Hot and Cold Baths at all hours daily, and Sundays until 10 o'clock, A. M.

SPECIAL CARE GIVEN TO LADIES' & CHILDREN'S HAIR CUTTING.

Artistic Manufacturer of Wigs, Hair Switches, and all Manner of Hair Work.

Cæsar, the Brilliant Boot Polisher, Always on Hand.

☞ EXPERIENCED AND SKILLED BARBERS ONLY EMPLOYED.◁

GOO KIM,

GENERAL CHINESE MERCHANT,

—

Nos. 65, 67, and 69 NUUANU STREET,

Also, cor. Fort and Hotel Sts., Honolulu,

And Branch Store at Kaiopihi, North Kohala, Hawaii,

— DEALER IN —

DRY GOODS,

CHINESE DRY GOODS,

Millinery Goods, Ladies & Gentlemen's Hats and Caps, Chinese Matttng, Saddles,

SILKS, AND SATIN GOODS, BOOTS, SHOES AND SLIPPERS,

All in Great Variety, and at Most Reasonable Prices.

Agent for Various Rice Plantations. Rice for Sale in Quantities
TO SUIT PURCHASERS.

53

In one of these recesses, or consecrated niches, they saw placed behind Buddha, a large painting representing a "lamb in the lap of the Son of Buddha." After a time wandering through the halls of the great temple, the high priest conducted His Majesty to a tasteful chamber, where refreshments were served in rare and unique style. Prominent upon a beautiful lacquered table was a large fish about 2 feet long, and showing all the natural bright colors, gold, ebony and scarlet of one of the most beautiful of the sclerodermes (the parrot fish that sports in Hawaiian waters). And yet the fish was well cooked, and these colors were the tints of wholesome condiments applied by the artist of Buddha's *cuisine*, after the culinary process was accomplished. A marvelous fish and birds and flowers of confectionery astonished the eyes of the travellers from the far Pacific islands,—and were presented to His Majesty to be forwarded to his island home. The high priest said that no one had sat at this table before except the Emperor or Mikado. His Majesty was seated upon a beautiful chair made of polished tortoise shell. The old high priest explained before eating, that this was the table of sacrifice of the Mikado; a sort of alter of thank offering. And a tray of small red papers, incense powder, and small fruits were placed before His Majesty, and a small portion of each were burned in an urn or censer; and after this form of Buddhist grace, the party fell too, and partook of a marvelous and most appretizing entertainment.

After leaving the temple His Majesty visited severals schools; one where little girls were taught embroidery; and some schools of boys; and the King was delighted with the bright appearance and cheerfulness of the little students of the several institutions.

Afterwards His Majesty and suite partook of tiffin, or lunch with His Excellency the Governor of Kobe.

The royal party on leaving Kobe proceeded by rail to Osaka distant 24 miles, and made a run at stage coach speed in 4 hours.

Here the same ceremonies were repeated by the Governor of the city, as at Kobe. A grand dinner was prepared; which however the royal party had to decline. From Osaka the royal party proceeded to Kioto; and thence to the beautiful city of Nangasaki.

At this point, the four princes, who had escorted the King; and who had waited on His Majesty during every hour of his stay in Japan, now took affectionate congee of their royal guest; who embarked March 22d on the Tokio Maru, that had been despatched expressly to wait on His Majesty, and transport the royal party to Shanghai.

ARRIVAL IN CHINA.

AT SHANGHAI.

His Majesty and suite arrived off the bar of the Shanghai roadstead on the 25th March and were takee thence by tug to the city, and were escorted by Mr. Jansen to the Astor Hotel. After a rest on the following day, His Majesty was waited upon by the Taotai, or chief magistrate of the city, and other Chinese dignitaries, and foreign representatives. The party took rides on the rigshaw, or one wheeled Chinese express at the rate of 10 cash, or one cent a mile. Witnessed a review, and were well entertained during a short stay at Shanghai.

On the 27th March the royal party embarked on the Pautah, one of the China Merchants Steamer Line; the King having been informed by the President of the Company, that by telegram from His Excellency Li Hung Chang the Viceroy residing at Tientsin, this vessel was placed at the disposal of His Majesty. The royal party steamed over the Yellow Sea, and arrived at the bar of the Bund, on the morning of 29th March.

E. B. THOMAS,

Contractor, Builder & Bricklayer,

P. O. BOX 117, HONOLULU, H. I.

Sewer | Setting

AND | OF

DRAIN | STEAM

WORK. | BOILERS.

Bake Ovens and Ranges, and all Kinds of Heating Apparatus attended to. Variegated Concrete Sidewalks laid in the most improved Modern Style. Having every facility at command on the most improved basis of Modern Art and Design, I wish to say that all work entrusted to my care will receive most careful attention, and I will guarantee to consummate all my undertaking in a substantial and workmanlike manner. Orders from the other Islands solicited.
Address P. O. Box 117, or call at Residence, 27 Alakea St.,

HONOLULU, H. I.

JNO. A. PALMER & CO.,

IMPORTING DRUGGISTS,

CORNER FORT AND MERCHANT STS, HONOLULU, H. I.

We have the Largest Stock of Drugs and Chemicals in the city.

A complete line of Patent Medicines and Proprietary Articles, embracing all the new and popular remedies, both American and European manufacture.

THE FINEST ASSORTMENT OF
TOILET ARTICLES & FANCY GOODS IN THE KINGDOM

A Large Stock of Optician's Goods.

PRICES REDUCED 50 PER CENT.

DROP IN.

AT TIENTSIN—VISITS THE VICEROY.

On the following day all the foreign representatives in the city waited on His Majesty on board the Pautah. On the 31st His Majesty and suite called upon the Viceroy Li Hang the Prime Minister and actual Ruler of China.

This distinguished official of the great Empire speaks little or no English, therefore His Majesty needed the assistance of an interpreter during a lengthy and highly interesting conversation. His Majesty with his thoughts ever patriotically occupied with the interests of his country, discussed on this occasion the great need of his little Kingdom, owing to the disproportion of sexes, of more women accompanying the emigration to his realm. The enlightened Viceroy expressed a high appreciation of His Majesty's patriotic anxiety in order to promote the increase and better social order of his island Kingdom, and said that should any farther emigration of the people of the Empire for the Sandwich Islands take place, he would favor all in his power, provided some provision was made by His Majesty's Government to assist female emigration.

The following day the 1st of April, the Viceroy waited upon His Majesty on board the Pautah. His Excellency and suite were conveyed in a splendid steam launch. They arrived on board punctual to appointment at noon, and remained several hours on board.

After the departure of the Viceroy, in the evening of the same day; the royal party went ashore, to partake of a grand Chinese dinner and soiree, given by the Viceroy in honor of His Majesty in the spacious building of the China Merchants Steamship Co. At 6.30 the arrival of the Viceroy was announced. A few minutes afterwards, as His Majesty and suite entered, three guns were fired. (The royal salute of China.) The feast was a marvel of Chinese ingenuity and luxury, and there was present on the occasion a splendid display of official Chinese dress, and of foreign uniforms, but no ladies. As the King noticed the absence of the gentler sex, His Majesty was informed by a distinguished mandarin that official etiquette forbade the presence of ladies on such an occasion; and in vindication of Chinese custom he said that Chinese ladies, who had no assemblies or Church meetings for mutual display and encounter, which Western civilization favored, but had to stay at home with their families, generally loved and spoke well of their neighboring sisters; and the worthy

8

mandarin wished to know if the ladies of His Majesty's capital were all animated by this excellent and amiable spirit. His Majesty's reply is not reported, but it was no doubt dictated by that wisdom and discretion requisite to meet the possible irony and insidious character of the enquiry.

RETURN TO SHANGHAI.

On the 2d April His Majesty and suite re-embarked on board the Pautah, and steaming back over the Yellow Sea, returned to Shanghai on the 6th April.

On the 9th April, His Majesty and suite left Shanghai per steamer, and arrived in Hongkong on the 12th April.

AT HONGKONG.

His Majesty King Kalakaua arrived on the 12th April. It was arranged that a banquet should be given in honor of His Majesty at Government House on Monday next. Immediately after the banquet His Majesty will hold a public reception, at which the Members of Council, Heads of Departments, Naval and Military Officers, Foreign Consuls, and the leading residents of the Colony, both ladies and gentlemen, will be introduced to His Majesty.

BANQUET AND RECEPTION.

His Excellency the Governor and Lady Hennessy gave a grand banquet in honor of His Majesty the King of Hawaii, after which a reception was held by His Majesty, which was numerously attended, about three hundred persons being present. Dancing commenced about half-past ten, His Majesty leading off Lady Hennessy, and was kept up till past midnight, to the strains of the Band of the 27th Inniskillings. The assemblage was a brilliant one and proved a great success, the gathering being truly cosmopolitan and representative.

VISIT TO KOWLOONG.

Yesterday morning, Mr. C. P. Chater, Deputy District Grand Master of the Freemasons of Hongkong, entertained His Majesty the King of Hawaii, and suite, His Excellency the Governor, and a large number of the residents at tiffin in his spacious bungalow at Kowloong, His Majesty King Kalakaua and suite and His Excellency Sir John Pope Hennessy, attended by his Private Secretary, Dr. Eitel, arrived about half-past one o'clock, and were received at the garden steps

WILDER & CO.,

Importers and Dealers in Lumber

—— AND ——

All Kinds of Building Materials.

IMPORTERS & DEALERS IN COAL

Honolulu, Oahu, H. I.

Steamer Likelike,

Regular Weekly Communication with the Islands of Maui and Hawaii.

Steamer Lehua,

Regular Weekly Communication with the Islands of Molokai and Maui.

Steamer Mokolii,

Regular Weekly Communication with Ports on the Windward side of Oahu.

HONOLULU ICE WORKS.

Office with Wilder & Co.

Ice always on hand, and Orders Promptly Filled.

AGENTS FOR THE

Mutual Life Insurance Company

OF NEW YORK.

by the hospitable host, who conducted them to the entrance of the banqueting room, where they were received with a ringing cheer by the assembled guests. About one hundred and forty guests sat down to an elegant and most bountiful repast. In the centre of the room were ranged Mr. Chater's numerous and handsome trophies of the turf, which presented a really magnificent *coup d'œil*. The distinguished guests having been seated in order of precedence, the tiffin proceeded. At its close Mr. Chater rose and in a few well chosen and apposite sentence proposed the health of His Majesty the King of Hawaii. The toast was received with great enthusiasm, the company drinking it in bumpers and giving three ringing cheers for their illustrious visitor. The King replied in a short but felicitous speech, in the course of which he said that though his kingdom had no commercial treaty with the Colony of Hongkong he should be glad to enter into one of friendship with it, and (referring to Mr. Chater's collection of racing cups) would feel pleasure in forwarding a cup to be contested for at the next annual races, and he had no doubt his friends in Hongkong would return the compliment and send one to Honolulu. A long continued outburst of applause followed this sally. His Majesty concluded by gracefully proposing the health of Her Majesty the Queen. The toast was received with fervent acclamation.

KING KALAKAUA IN SIAM.

His Majesty and suite took passage from Hongkong to Bangkok. Passing over an uneventful voyage, they arrived at the bar of the Menam, the great river of Siam, on the morning of the 26th April. On entering the river, the steam yacht of the King of Siam was seen approaching, and shortly afterwards a twelve-oared boat carrying the flag of the White Elephant came alongside, carrying an officer of His Majesty's household, commissioned to tender to King Kalakaua the hospitalities of his brother of Siam. The invitation was accompanied by expressions of regret on the part of His Majesty that he had not received sufficiently early notice of the arrival of his royal visitor to allow of his meeting him in person at the river bar. Another boat accompanied that of the Envoy, carrying His Siamese Majesty's Aide-de-Camp, DISSAWORKA-MARU. Salutations were exchanged, and the whole party proceeded on board the yacht, which is described as " a beautiful boat," and made in her the voyage up the Menam to Bangkok, a distance of about twenty miles. The manner in which this yacht was found and fitted seems to have excited the admiration of all the party. Under an awning, so tasteful in its character as to attract attention even among so many novelties, cool drinks and delicious liquors had been provided in profusion, with the wellcome accompaniment of the choicest Manila and Siamese cheroots.

ARRIVAL IN BANGKOK.

Bangkok, as our party steamed through it under these luxurious circumstances proved highly interesting. Many of its peculiarities which attracted their notice are common to other river-side cities of Eastern Asia, but Bangkok has a quaint character of its own, which makes it worthy of a more prolonged visit, than our travellers could pay. The river divides the city, and on either side, built out on slender piles into the stream itself, stores of every description line the shores, whilst the river itself is alive with boats and canoes. The curiously designed pagodas, the temples with their tile-lined fronts, brilliant with gilding and silvering, burnished so that they reflect the rays of a truly tropical sun with a dazzle which obliges the eye to turn elsewhere, the green and trim gardens full of the brightest flowers, made a picture which none of the party will soon forget.

It was half-past six before the voyage up the river came to an end. A splendid large boat manned by 24 oarsmen took the royal party ashore, and from the landing they were conveyed in sedan chairs to the Palace of one of the Princes; a regiment of infantay lining the way, and several royal vessels and men-of-war lying in the river, and firing salutes, Here His Hawaiian Majesty was received in truly royal style. By a splendid marble staircase flanked by rows of polished granite columns, His Majesty entered an antechamber, some eighty feet in length, with floors in mosaic of marble, and furniture of ebony. Statues, vases, and other products of the highest order of Western art, and paintings by European masters lined the apartment, whilst damasks, hanging richly embroidered in gold, served to conceal the multitude of guards and servants who were in attendance.

The following day at 2 p. m. had been fixed for the reception of King KALAKAUA by his royal brother of Siam. Accompanied by his suite and by Prince DISSAWORKUMARU, His Majesty was conveyed to the Palace. This building is described as a masterpiece of architecture; built of highly polished marble, the inner walls inlaid with precious stones, the floors a mosaic of colored marbles. The King of Siam is a

64

ED. HOFFMAN, M. D.

IMPORTER OF THE BEST AND

Genuine Drugs, Perfumery and Toilet Articles,

DIRECT FROM THE MOST

CELEBRATED MANUFACTORIES IN

Europe and the United States.

EVERY ARTICLE

Guaranteed of the Purest Quality,

AND SOLD AT VERY LOW PRICES.

Store on Merchant Street, Honolulu, H. I.

BISMARKS'
FASHION STABLES

NEXT TO NO. 2 ENGINE CO. HOUSE

ENTRANCE

No. 3 Union St.

And No. 99 Hotel St.

HONOLULU, H. I

FIRST CLASS SADDLE HORSES

SINGLE & DOUBLE CARRIAGES,

— AND —

Buggies to Rent at any Hour of the Day or Night

Our Expresses Nos. 7, 9, 32, 34, 52, 91 and 193

Are the finest and most comfortable Riding Vehicles in the city.

All Orders Promptly Attended to.   Terms Reasonable.

Telephone No. 148, on the Premises.

man of about 27 years of age, with a firm resolute face, no beard, a keen eye and massive forehead. He was dressed for the occasion in a tunic of gold brocade, with the silk garment, worn by all Siamese of rank, wound round his legs, leaving, as is their custom, a little bare at the back of the knee. He was decorated with a multitude of insignia of various orders, and his sword belt glittered with diamonds, rubies and sapphires. His Siamese Majesty was attended by His Minister of Foreign Affairs, Chow Phya Bhanuwougse, and forty other high officers of state.

His Siamese Majesty greeted the Hawaiian King and, through his interpreter, asked after his health and expressed his regret that, through shortness of notice, he was not better prepared for His Majesty's reception. King Kalakaua was conducted to a seat, but Siamese etiquette bade all others remain standing. After a short conversation His Siamese Majesty retired with a ceremonious farewell.

At four o'clock in the afternoon of the 28th, the arrival of a troop of cavalry announced the approach of His Siamese Majesty to return the visit of King Kalakaua. He came in a carriage, which to the eyes of his guests appeared to be all of gold, drawn by four horses. His Majesty and two Ministers who were in attendance on him, alighted and were received at the threshold of the palace by King Kalakaua. Congratulations were exchanged and as on the occasion of their former meeting only the two monarchs were seated

In true Oriental style the royal host did not allow his guest to depart without presents suitable to his rank. In the evening a State dinner was given at the palace, and at eleven the following morning a regretful leave was taken of Bangkok, its fairy-like palaces and temples, its hospitable monarch, and the kindly men of rank who had vied with their sovereign in his endeavor to make the stay of their visitors from the lonely Isles of the Pacific as delightful as a dream. A superb barge manned by 24 oarsmen, was ready to receive the royal traveller, and after a pull of 15 minutes landed the King and suite on the steamer Bangkok. The royal Hawaiian standard was hoisted at the main; the troops on shore fired a salute; and the multitudes of hospitable Siamese gave prolonged, and rousing cheers, as the royal travelling party steamed away down the Menam.

THE KING IN SINGAPORE.

His Majesty, accompanied by his suite and Mr. Herwig, the Hawaiian Consul, landed about a quarter past 10 A. M. at Johnston's Pier, and then walked down to the Hotel de

9

l'Europe where the King is staying. A large crowd of natives and Europeans witnessed His Majesty's landing and manifested a lively and respectful curiosity. Johnston's Pier was most tastefully decorated with palms and evergreen plants, and the large number of flags, with the Hawaiian national flag on a large pole, added greatly to the general effect.

On Saturday H. E. the Governor Sir Frederick A. Weld drove down to town with his four-in-hand, in full uniform, and returned the call of H. M. the King of the Hawaiian Islands. Afterwards His Majesty and suite drove with His Ex. to the reservoir, with which His Majesty expressed himself highly pleased. Yesterday afternoon His Majesty held a reception at Government House, when many officials and other gentlemen and ladies were presented. In the evening His Excellency and Lady Weld gave a large official dinner in honor of His Majesty, at which Admiral Aslambegoff and Prince Torlonia were also present.

RECEPTION BY THE SULTAN OF JOHORE.

During the stay at Singapore, His Majesty received some distinguished royal courtesy at the hands of the Sultan, or Maharajah of Johore, whose palace is distant forty miles from Singapore. His Majesty the King having accepted an invitation to visit His Highness the Maharajah, the steam launch of the Prince was despatched to Singapore, and on the morning of 10th May conveyed the royal traveller to the palace of Istana. Our travellers were astonished and delighted with the fine architecture and royal appointments of the palace. Sultan Abubakr and his courtiers have marked Hawaiian types of features, and the Malay Prince was recognized as presenting a striking likeness to the late Hawaiian Prince Leleiohoku. The ladies of the Court of Istana are spoken of in terms of enthusiastic eulogy.

Costly furniture and bricabac adorn this noble palace, the hospitality of which was extended so royally to our King, that we are placed under deep obligation by the Malay Sultan, as we have been by a Japanese Emperor, a Siamese King, and a Chinese Viceroy.

After a stay of seven days in Singapore, His Majesty King KALAKAUA took his departure for Calcutta *en route* to Europe the 12th May by the B. I. S. N. Co.'s steamer *Mecca*, Captain Thomson.

GEORGE LUCAS,

CONTRACTOR AND BUILDER,

HONOLULU STEAM PLANING MILLS,

Nos. 36 & 38 Fort Street.

MANUFACTURER OF ALL KINDS OF

Mouldings,      *Brackets,*

Window Frames   *Blinds,*

Sashes,   *Doors.*

And all Kinds of Wood-work Finish.

TURNING, SCROLL AND BAND SAWING.

PLANING AND SAWING.
MORTICING & TENANTING.

My Extensive Improvements on my Mills together with additional Machinery of Modern Invention and Skillful Mechanics employed, enable me to carry on my business with greater facilities than ever, and on Most Reasonable Terms.

ORDERS FROM THE OTHER ISLANDS SOLICITED,

ALL WORK PROMPTLY ATTENDED TO and GUARANTEED.

THE PALACE.

HOTEL STREET, NEAR FORT.

THE ICE CREAM PARLORS

Of this Establishment are Neatly Fitted Up, and are Quite
Private. Only the

PUREST ICED CREAMS

SUPPLIED.

—

POLITE AND GENTLEMANLY WAITERS.

—

ICED CORDIALS AND AERATED WATERS ALWAYS ON HAND.

ICED CREAMS

Supplied to Parties on Short Notice.

——

The Billiard Parlors are fitted up with

FIRST-CLASS TABLES.

NOTHING BUT THE BEST BRANDS OF

TOBACCO & CIGARS

KEPT ON HAND.

—

S. NOWLEIN, Proprietor.

IN EGYPT.

After a rapid trip across the Indian Peninsular His Majesty arrived at Suez on the morning of Monday, June 20th and found a special train, provided by the hospitality of the Khedive, ready to convey him to Cairo. After spending a few days there and visiting the Pyramids and other objects of interest, His Majesty went forward ;to Alexandria where he was received with much state by the Khedive. On the night of Friday, June 26th, a grand State Ball was given in honor of the King at the vice-regal palace. It was attended by the Abyssinian Ambassador, the Consular corps and the leading residents, Egyptian and foreign, of Cairo and Alexandria. On the following morning the Khedive's barge, with the Hawaiian Royal Standard flying, took His Majesty on board the steamer "Asia" bound for Naples and the Egyptian flagship "Mahomed Ali" fire a royal salute as the King embarked. During his stay at Cairo, His Majesty visited the Grand Orient of Egypt when the degree of Hon. Grand Master of the Grand Orient was conferred upon him. On this occasion His Majesty delivered a lengthy address on some of the mysteries of the craft and of the great Pyramid which has been published at length in the P. C. ADVERTISER of August 13th.

THROUGH ITALY.

On landing at Naples His Majesty was received by the Prefect of that city, the military Commandant, and the Admiral of the station; and on the following day July 1st, had an interview with King Humberto at the royal country seat at Capo di Monte. Proceeding the next day to Rome, His Majesty was on the Sunday received by His Holiness the Pope who received the King very kindly and asked many questions about the Hawaiian Kingdom and people. The evening and the early part of the following day were spent in visiting some of the chief points of interest in the Eternal city.

IN ENGLAND.

Attracted by a great Volunteer Review which was to be held on the following Saturday at Windsor. His Majesty left Rome on the 4th and made a rapid journey direct to London, where he arrived on the evening of the 6th. Here apartments had been prepared for the King and his suite at Claridge's Hotel at the cost of Her Majesty the Queen, and one of the royal Carriages and the royal box at the Italian

Opera House were also placed at His Majesty's disposal. His Majesty's stay in London was prolonged until a late hour on the 24th and was one continual round of receptions, visiting and sight seeing. H. R. H. the Prince of Wales would appear to have devoted himself to the task of rendering the King's visit to England one of the most pleasant memories of his future life. On Saturday July 9th the King visited the grand Volunteer Review in Windsor Park travelling there and back in a carriage and four. The troops to the number of 55,000, were reviewed in the presence of the Queen. On the Monday following His Majesty lunched with the Earl and Countess Granville, meeting there the Rt. Hon. W. E. Gladstone, Lord Kimberly, Sir Charles W. Dilke, and many other distinguished guests, and then proceeded to Windsor to be presented to Her Majesty Queen Victoria. The King was presented by Earl Granville and was received in a more than usually gracious manner by Her Majesty who gave him her hand, and making him be seated near her chatted pleasantly with him on several topics.

On July 13th His Majesty was present at a garden party at Fulham, the residence of the Archbishop of Canterbury, and at a conversazione given by Earl and Countess Spencer at the South Kensington Museum. On the 4th the King was at a garden party at Marlborough House given by the Prince and Princess of Wales to the Queen. A most distinguished company was present on this occasion, including the Crown Prince and Princess of Germany with the Princess Victoria, Sophia and Margaret of Prussia, the Duke and Duchess of Connaught, Prince and Princess Christian of Schleswig-Holstein, the Princess Louise (Marchioness of Lorne), the Duke of Cambridge, Princess Mary Adelaide (Duchess of Teck) and the Duke of Teck. The list of the other invited guests, comprising the entire diplomatic body and their ladies, all prominent members of the aristocracy, the army, the navy, bar, church, etc., filled four columns of small print in the *Morning Post*. The evening was spent by His Majesty at the House of Commons, and the next evening he was present at a grand ball given at Hyde Park Barracks by the officers of the 2nd Life Guards. On Saturday the King was the guest of the Lord Mayor at a dinner party given to the Prince of Wales, on which occasion he replied very happily when his health was proposed.

Sunday July 7 was spent at Normanhurst Court, the seat of Sir Thomas Brassey. On the following Tuesday, Lady Alfred Paget gave a ball in His Majesty's honor. Wednesday evening was devoted to the Anniversary Banquet at the

Trinity House, at which the Prince of Wales presided, when the toast of His Majesty's health was enthusiastically responded to. The remainder of the week was devoted to sightseeing and receiving and paying visits. On Sunday, July 24, after taking leave of the Prince and Princess of Wales (the Court was absent at Osborne) His Majesty left London for the Continent. Before his departure he received from the Queen the decoration of Honorary Member of the First Class of Knights Grand Cross of the Order of St. Michael and St· George.

AT BRUSSELS.

His Majesty was received and feted by Count de Carmart d'Hamale Consul General for this Kingdom in Belgium. Wednesday and part of Thursday were occupied by sightseeing. On the afternoon of the latter day His Majesty King Leopold II who had been detained at the National fetes at Liege paid a state visit to the King which was returned the same day. The two monarchs engaged in an interesting and very cordial conversation and parted mutually delighted with one another.

IN GERMANY.

His Majesty travelled direct from Brussels to Berlin by rail, with only a break of three hours at Cologne, and arrived at the capital of Germany at a late hour on the 30th. During his six days stay in Berlin the King was "lionized over the capital; before his hotel and at all points visited by him large crowds continually assembled to see and greet the foreign sovereign; great military spectacles were arranged for him; and interviews took place with all the Royal Princes then at Berlin." The Crown Prince was in London where His Majesty had already met and received much attention from him. The Emperor of Germany was absent at Gastein. Among the sights of Berlin, the military displays got up especially for His Majesty's gratification seem to have most particulary attrcted the notice of the King being perfect of their kind and being the performances of troops believed to be the best disciplined in the world. On Wednesday August 2d, the King dined at Potsdam with Prince Charles when there were also present the Prince and Princess William, Prince Frederick Charles, the "Red Prince" and celebrated cavalry leader, and the Prince and Princess of Meiningen, the Crown Prince's son-in-law and daughter. The same evening His Majesty left for Essen to visit the cannon and machine foundries of Herr Krupp.

On the 4th His Majesty left Berlin and arrived

AT VIENNA

on the evening of the following day and was officially received by Field Marshal Baron von Tiller representing the Emperor, and was conducted to apartments at the Imperial Hotel which had just previously been occupied by the King of Denmark. The Emperor of Austria was absent travelling in Bavaria but at his request the Archduke Albrecht went expressly to Vienna to have an interview with the King. His Majesty remained four days in Vienna where he was scrupuluously entertained and visited all the chief objects of interest in that delightful city and its environs and from thence returned to Paris.

AT PARIS.

His Majesty's arrival was unannounced and therefore private. There being at the time no Hawaiian Consul in Paris, Count Carmart d'Hamale went especially from Brussels to attend upon His Majesty. The President was absent from the capital but M. Barthelemy de St. Hilaire, Minister of Foreign Affairs, waited upon the King and welcomed him in the name of the French Government. The President's aide de camp also called on behalf of M. Grevy, to express the hope that a future meeting might be arranged. His Majesty remained at Paris until Aug. 15th, engaged in receiving innumerable visits and in sight-seeing. He was present at the International Electrical Exhibition and was greatly interested in what he saw there. Whilst at Paris he received an autograph letter from the King of the Belgians, accompanying the Grand Cross and Ribbon of the Order of Leopold.

The following is but a short summary of His Majesty's subsequent movements before returning to England. August 17th, arrival at the Escurial, 7 a. m.., and inspection of this ancient palace of Spanish Royalty; at 11, arrival at Madrid, at Hotel de la Paix; calls by State Officials, at 8 p. m., departure for Portogal; at frontier, reception by guards of honor. August 19th, 6 a. m., at Lisbon, State reception at depot by 2nd Infantry regiment as guards of honor, military band playing Hawaiian anthem, in four royal carriages with fore-riders and escort of a squadron of cavalry, to Hotel Braganza, 3 p. m., meeting with King Louis of Portugal and return visit at half-past 4. When His Majesty was invested with the Grand Cross of the Conception and in return conferred the Order of Kamehameha on King Louis. August 20th, visit to royal country seat at Cintra, at 6 p. m., dinner with the King. August 21st, visit to Don Ferdinand, the King's father. August 22, at 2 p. m., farewell visit to the King, to a bull fight, departure for Spain at 6 p. m., with escorts of officials and cavalry. August 24, arrival at Madrid, at 6 a. m.; call by Secretary of Foreign Affairs as representative of the King, absent travelling in Galicia; visits to picture gallery and Retiro Park, in evening to theatre. August 25, visit to military barracks, Royal Castle stables, at 5 p. m., departure for France. August 27, arrival at Paris, 6 a. m., to Continental hotel. August 28, visits to Hotel des Invalides and Napoleon's tomb, private dinner in evening and to concert. August 29th, visit to Louvre and Art Museum, evening to opera, calls by the Prince of Orange, Prince Alexander of the Netherlands. August 30th, visit to the great Nickel works of Count Hankar; reception of farewell visits. From Paris forwarded to Charles I of Roumania on his assumption of the title of King the Grand Cross df the Order of Kamehameha. Departure for London and arrive there at 6 a. m. on Aug. 31st. Sept. 1st. Visit to St. Paul's and the tombs of Wellington and Nelson. Sept. 2nd. To the Tower of London. Presentation to His Majesty by the Swedish Charge d'Affairs of the insignia of the Holy Cross of Vasa. Sept. 3d. Visit to the Blenheim Gun and Small Arms Works. Sunday, Sept. 4th. His Majesty attended service at St. Paul's. Sept. 5th. Visit to Woolwich Arsenal, where the manufacture of wheels by machinery and the making of heavy shells were exhibited to His Majesty. The reserve equipment of harness for 10,000 horses was greatly admired by the King. Sept. 6tth. Farewell visit to Their Royal Highnesses the Prince and Princess of Wales at Malborough House. Departure for Scotland by the night express. Sept. 7th. Received at Glasgow by Councillor W. Renny Watson; visit to the leading shipbuilding yards of the Clyde; entertained at dinner by the Lord Provost and Baillies. Sept. 8th. Visit to Loch Lomond and trip on the Clyde from Arrochas to Glasgow. Sept. 9th. Departure for Edinburgh. Warm reception there by the Lord Provost and Municipal Officers. Visit to Mr. R. A. Scott Macfie at Dreghorn Castle. Sept 10th. Planting Commemoration trees at Dreghorn. Drive to Edinburgh by way of Hunter's Tryst Avenue and Corniston, and the Borestone at Morningside. Drive to Sampson's Ribs, Arthur's Seat and Holyrood ; thence to the Freemason's Hall to attend special meeting of Grand Conclave of Scotland of the order of the Red Cross of Constantine called to confer on His Majesty the rank of Knight Grand Cross of the Order; entertained at luncheon by Dr. Bishop; departure from Edinburg for Rufford Park, the seat of Sir Thomas Hesketh, where His Majesty remained until Monday morning. Sept.

12th. Arrived at Liverpool; reception by the Mayor and other officials; visits to St. George's Hall, the docks and other places of interest; trip on the Mersey; State dinner to His Majesty at the Town Hall. Sept. 13th. Embarkation on the Steamer Celtic for New York.

IN AMERICA.

Sept. 23rd, The King landed from the Celtic; His Majesty sent a letter expressing sympathy to Mrs. Garfield and despatched Mr. E. H. Allen, His Majesty's Consul at New York, to Washington, to represent him at the funeral of the late President. The following day was spent in private at Coney Island. His Majesty made a call upon President Arthur and subsequently proceeded to the Hampton Institute, Virginia, to pay a visit to General Armstrong and observe his work there. He was at Cincinnati on October 3rd and passed Omaha on the 7th by the overland train bound for San Francisco, where he would arrive on the 11th. It is expected that he would sail for Honolulu in the Pacific Mail Steamer Australia and that he will arrive here at an early hour on Monday, Oct. 31st;

HIS LOYAL PEOPLE EXPECTING HIM.

—————

GOD SAVE THE KING.

—————

HIS MAJESTY'S SUITE.

—————

WM. N. ARMSTRONG, Commissioner of Immigration.

CHARLES H. JUDD, Lord Chamberlain.

GEORGE W. MACFARLANE, Aide de Camp.

HERR ROB'T VON OEHLHAFFEN, Personal Attendant.

JOHN BOWLER

PLAIN, ORNAMENTAL & STUCCO PLASTERER

Artificial Stone Sidewalks Laid,
Cementing in all its Branches,
Whitening, Kalsomining & Jobbing,

PROMPTLY ATTENDED TO.

Asbestos Steam Pipe and Boiler Covering

DONE IN THE BEST MANNER

AND BY

Experienced Workmen

As to my ability to perform work in my Line, I beg to refer the Public generally to the residences of Hon. Sam'l G. Wilder, H. H. Ruth Keelikolani, Hon. C. H. Judd, His Majesty's Palace and others.

Orders from the Other Islands Promptly Attended To.

☞ Leave Orders with J. E. WISEMAN, HIGGINS & JESSETT, Carriage Builders, or at the ADVERTISER OFFICE.

·

www.ingramcontent.com/pod-product-compliance
Lightning Source LLC
Chambersburg PA
CBHW020235090426
42735CB00010B/1706